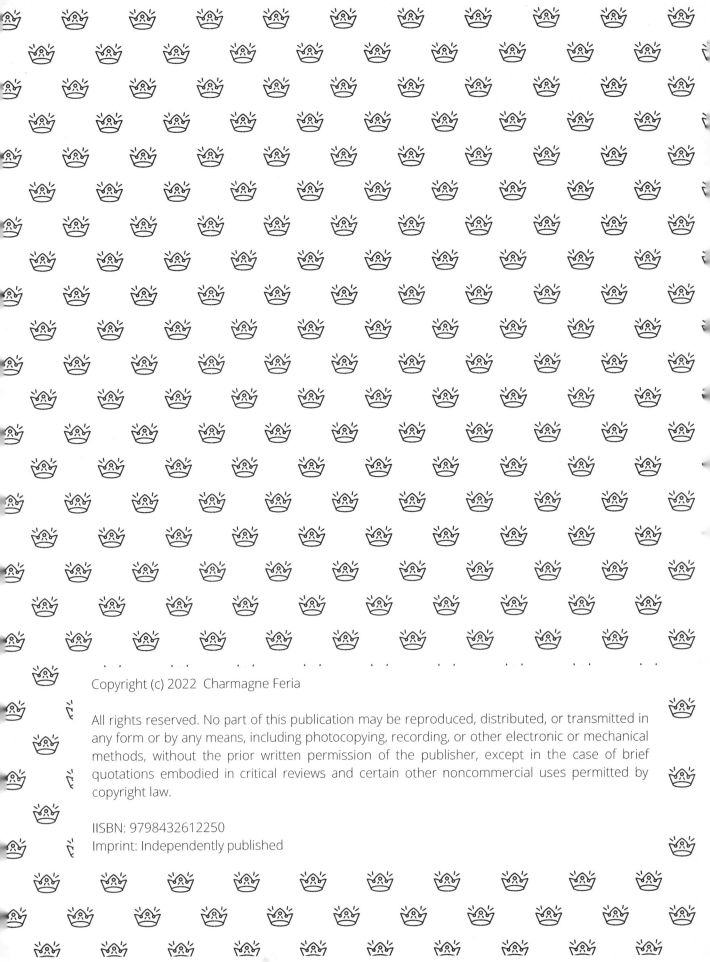

IISBN: 9798432612250
Imprint: Independently published

The Platinum Jubilee of Queen Elizabeth II

The Platinum Jubilee of Elizabeth II marks the 70th anniversary of the accession of Queen Elizabeth II on 6 February 1952.

Events and initiatives will take place throughout 2022 within the United Kingdom, the Realms and the Commonwealth, culminating in a four day UK bank holiday weekend from Thursday 2nd to Sunday 5th June.

The events described in the pages of this journal are based on the official events published at the Platinum Jubilee website at (https://platinumjubilee.gov.uk). Various other events are held that are not featured in this publication.

Date: _____

Date: _____

Date: _____

Date: _____

_____

_____

_____

_____

_____

_____

_____

_____

_____

_____

_____

_____

_____

_____

_____

_____

The Queen's Accession Day message
Published 5 February 2022

Tomorrow, 6th February, marks the 70th anniversary of my Accession in 1952. It is a day that, even after 70 years, I still remember as much for the death of my father, King George VI, as for the start of my reign.

As we mark this anniversary, it gives me pleasure to renew to you the pledge I gave in 1947 that my life will always be devoted to your service.

As I look ahead with a sense of hope and optimism to the year of my Platinum Jubilee, I am reminded of how much we can be thankful for. These last seven decades have seen extraordinary progress socially, technologically and culturally that have benefitted us all; and I am confident that the future will offer similar opportunities to us and especially to the younger generations in the United Kingdom and throughout the Commonwealth.

I am fortunate to have had the steadfast and loving support of my family.

I was blessed that in Prince Philip I had a partner willing to carry out the role of consort and unselfishly make the sacrifices that go with it. It is a role I saw my own mother perform during my father's reign.

This anniversary also affords me a time to reflect on the goodwill shown to me by people of all nationalities, faiths and ages in this country and around the world over these years. I would like to express my thanks to you all for your support. I remain eternally grateful for, and humbled by, the loyalty and affection that you continue to give me. And when, in the fullness of time, my son Charles becomes King, I know you will give him and his wife Camilla the same support that you have given me; and it is my sincere wish that, when that time comes, Camilla will be known as Queen Consort as she continues her own loyal service.

And so as I look forward to continuing to serve you with all my heart, I hope this Jubilee will bring together families and friends, neighbours and communities – after some difficult times for so many of us – in order to enjoy the celebrations and to reflect on the positive developments in our day-to-day lives that have so happily coincided with my reign.

Source: https://www.royal.uk/queens-accession-day-message

Date:_____

Date:_____

Date:_____

The Queen's Green Canopy

Plant a tree to celebrate the Platinum Jubilee. The Queen's Green Canopy (QGC) invites people from across the United Kingdom to "Plant a Tree for the Jubilee" during the official planting season between October to March in honour of The Queen's leadership of the Nation. The Queen's Green Canopy will dedicate a network of 70 Ancient Woodlands across the United Kingdom and identify 70 Ancient Trees to celebrate Her Majesty's 70 years of service. Over 60,000 trees have already been planted in the UK through the project in the two months since the planting season began.

Date: _____

Date: _____

Date:_____

The Platinum Pudding Competition

It does not matter whether you are a professional baker, a hobbyist or someone who just likes to bake puddings. Bake a pudding that is not only worthy of the Queen but is also simple enough to recreate for the celebrations and you will take home the prize. Fortnum & Mason set out to find the winning pudding that will be a sweet part of the celebrations marking Her Majesty's 70 years as Monarch. The winner will be invited to be at the centre of the celebrations.

Date:_____

Date:_____

Date: _____

Queen's Birthday Parade (Trooping the Colour)

It's time for a parade! The Queen's Birthday Parade will involve over 1,400 soldiers, 200 horses and 400 musicians. Kicking off at Buckingham Palace, the parade will move down The Mall to Horse Guard's Parade, joined by Members of the Royal Family on horseback and in carriages. There will be a traditional RAF fly-past, watched by The Queen and Members of the Royal Family from the Buckingham Palace balcony.

Date: _____

Date:_____

Date: _____

Platinum Jubilee Beacons

Light 'em up! The lighting of the beacons is the first community event in the four day celebrations. Thousands of beacons will be lighted by communities, charities and different groups throughout the regions of the UK, Channel Islands, Isle of Man and UK Overseas Territories. Fifty four 54 beacons will be lit in all capital cities of the Commonwealth while the Principal Beacon will be lit   at Buckingham Palace   on the 2nd June. There are three kinds of official beacons: a free standing gas fuelled beacon, a beacon brazier with a metal shield, and a bonfire beacon.

Date: _____

Date: _____

Date: _____

Service of Thanksgiving

On Friday 3rd June, a Service of Thanksgiving for The Queen's reign will be held at St Paul's Cathedral at St. Paul's Churchyard, London. The service will not be open to the public.

Date:_____

Date:_____

Date: _____

The Derby at Epsom Downs

The 2022 Cazoo Derby at Epsom Downs Racecourse will be held on Friday 3rd June and Saturday 4th June 2022. It features the Cazoo Oaks – first run in 1779 – and the Cazoo Derby – first run a year later and the world's most famous Flat horse race. The derby is significant to Her Majesty because she achieved her best result to date, with her horse Aureole finishing second to Pinza, three days after Her Majesty's Coronation, on Saturday 6th June 1953. The Queen will attend the derby at Epsom Downs on Saturday 4th June 2022.

Date:_____

Date:_____

Date: _____

Platinum Party at the Palace

The Royal Family and the BBC will host a special live concert from Buckingham Palace on Saturday, 4th June 2022, which will bring together some of the world's biggest entertainment stars to perform for Her Majesty The Queen. The event will celebrate some of the most significant cultural moments from The Queen's seven decade reign. It will feature a full, live orchestra and state-of-the-art technology. It is open to the public, but advance booking is required.

Date:_____

Date:_____

Date: _____

The Big Jubilee Lunch

On Sunday, 5th June, the Big Jubilee Lunch will be held. It is a way to share friendship, food and fun within the community. There will be street parties, picnic, tea and cake or a garden barbeque. Over 1,400 people all over the country have registered to host Big Jubilee Lunches so far.

Date:_____

Date: _____

Date: _____

Royal Collection Trust

Three special displays featuring the Accession, the Coronation and Jubilees will be staged at the official royal residences from July 2022. The portraits of Her Majesty The Queen between 1953 and 1956, alongside items of personal jewellery worn for the sittings will be on display at the Summer Opening of the State Rooms at Buckingham Palace. The Queen's Coronation Dress and Robe of Estate for her Coronation at Westminster Abbey on 2 June 1953 will be featured at Windsor Castle. The outfits worn by Her Majesty to celebrate the Silver, Golden and Diamond Jubilees will be available for viewing at the Palace of Holyroodhouse.

Date:_____

Date: _____

Date: _____

The Platinum Jubilee Pageant

The Platinum Jubilee Pageant will be hosted in London. Featuring talents from every part of the United Kingdom and across the Commonwealth, it will combine theatre arts, music, circus, costumes and will feature cutting-edge visual technology. The 'River of Hope' section is a procession of two hundred silk flags down The Mall, appearing like a moving river. The silk flags will feature artwork created by primary and secondary school children, that depict their hopes and aspirations for the planet over the next 70 years. The artwork for the flags will focus on climate change and the children's messages for the future.

Date: _____

Date: _____

Date: _____

The Platinum Jubilee Celebration

The Platinum Jubilee Celebration from 12th -15th May consists of over 500 horses and 1,000 performers in a 90-minute piece of arena theatre that will include actors and artists, musicians, international military displays, dancers and global equestrian displays. The show will highlight the events through history from Elizabeth I to the present day.

Date:_____

Date: _____

Date: _____

Windsor Castle, Berkshire

Date: _____

Date:_____

Date: _____

Palace of Holyroodhouse,
Edinburgh, United Kingdom

Date:_____

Date: _____

Date:_____

Kensington Palace, London

Date: _____

Date: _____

Date: _____

Tower Bridge, London

Date: _____

Date: _____

Date: _____

Victoria Memorial
in front of Buckingham Palace

Date: _____

Date: _____

Date: _____

Date: _____

Date: _____

Date: _____

Date:_____

Date: _____

Date:_____

Date: _____

Date: _____

Date: _____

Date: _____

Date: _____

Date: _____

Date: _____

Date:_____

Date: _____

Date: _____

Date:_____

Date: _____

Date: _____

Date: _____

Date:_____

Date: _____

Printed in Great Britain
by Amazon

79763384R10059